The Problem Solver

The Problem Solver

Donny Blumingburg

J. Kenkade
PUBLISHING®
LITTLE ROCK, ARKANSAS

J. Kenkade Publishing
6104 Forbing Rd
Little Rock, AR 72209
www.jkenkadepublishing.com
Facebook.com/jkenkadepublishing

J. Kenkade Publishing is a registered trademark.

Printed in the United States of America
ISBN 978-1-955186-00-1

Table of Contents

FOREWARD

It is with great honor that I commend the author, Donny Blumingburg, and his Kingdom results in his new book, *The Problem Solver*. There are many books of information and life stories that are necessary to read. However, Pastor Donny has navigated us through both a quick read and an in-depth study to awaken the saints of God in their uniqueness, anointing, and call of God upon their lives. *The Problem Solver* will redirect and challenge one's thinking about themselves and their purpose in their transformed life in Christ. You are here on this earth for a purpose, and God wants you to walk in the fullness of that purpose. Donny has done an excellent job producing a book that will help the reader discover and activate their purpose in Christ Jesus.

This book is a must for every person, saved and unsaved alike, to help you get back on track with God's call and purpose in your life. This is an excellent tool for a group study as well as a classroom study.

Thank you, Pastor Donny, for this masterful work to advance the Church, the Ecclesia, into its meaningful purpose. May you write many more books to advance the Kingdom of God.

Love and blessings,

Apostle Dr. M. Leon Walters
Author of *Unity's Power As One*, *Reset With No Regret*, and *Spiritual Fathering*

ACKNOWLEDGEMENTS

To every leader in my life, I couldn't have done this without you. Thank you for investing in me and seeing in me what I couldn't see in myself.

And I saved the best for last. To my wife, Prophetess Angela Blumingburg, a great and virtuous woman of God. Thank you for your understanding and great support. You have always been by my side through thick and thin. You are my best friend. You are my delight, and you share in the youth of my heart. When I was a failure, you saw a bright future. You always looked beyond my present defeat and saw that I was worth sticking with. When I was broke and had not a dime, you always saw greatness in me. Other than God, you are my greatest treasure. Go forth! You have a calling and anointing all your own apart from me. Thank you for sticking with me twenty plus years of knowing me through every stage of growth.

INTRODUCTION

It was about mid-July as I sat on the couch in meditation, looking through some prophetic journals that stretched back multiple years. As I read through them, I began to see the love of God manifested. These were journals of information that God spoke into my life concerning my walk with Him and my destiny. As I looked back, I could see the tender, loving care of a real God who fearfully and carefully took me by the hand and began to impart Himself into my life years ago.

During that time, I came in contact with a living God who came after me. I can honestly say that God deserves all the credit for me being His. Most people feel this great void of emptiness before they run after God. I was minding my own business when the Spirit of God came after me rather than me coming after Him. He came in hot pursuit of my life.

"The Lord hath appeared of old unto me, saying, Yea, I have loved thee with an everlasting love: therefore with lovingkindness have I drawn thee."
Jeremiah 31:3

Genesis 1:2 states, "And the earth was without form, and void; and darkness was upon the face of the deep. And the Spirit of God moved upon the face of the waters."

The above scripture is an exact picture of how my life was: void and empty. I had no clue about destiny or anything like that. I had no clue of what it meant to be in relationship with God. When you're in a state of being blinded by the enemy, you can't see your true state and need for a Savior. I was without form, having no structure in my life, no godly jurisdiction, and no purpose. But the Spirit of God began to move mightily in my broken life. I had no idea that God wanted to use me. I knew that there was a God, but I only knew Him religiously, going to church every Sunday with no change ever taking place in my life.

There is more to being a Christian than dressing up and putting on a "church face" every Sunday and living for satan every other waking day of your life. But there is hope. If God moved in my life, bringing positive change, He will do it for you. God has a plan for your life. There are some things that God pre-planned for your life. There are things that God wants you to accomplish. God wants you to affect your generation after He has brought positive change for you. Do you really know that God wants to use you? God wants to use common, ordinary people just like you to carry out His plan. God has a plan that He wants to propagate here on Earth! And God eagerly desires to use you to birth His plan.

*"For when we were yet without strength,
in due time Christ died for the ungodly."*
Romans 5:6

*"But God commendeth his love toward us, in that,
while we were yet sinners, Christ died for us."*
Romans 5:8

As mentioned in the beginning, I began meditating on years of information God had spoken into my life. Questions began to swell in my spirit. What was the reason for the prophesies spoken over my life? And what was the reason God invested so much in me the last twenty years of my life, and so vigorously, in order to train me? God began to speak to me. God told me that the last twenty plus years of my life had been for His impartation to the body of Christ. I have been in training to do His will so that God could use me to be a solution here on Earth. God began to awaken the desire in my heart to write.

In this writing, I will endeavor to answer many questions and solve some problems. Why are you here? Why are you anointed? Is there more to God? Also, why are so

many leaders falling from grace and ministry? What is the purpose for the anointing on
your life and why is leadership so important?

Chapter 1

†

The Genesis

You are created to be a problem solver for Almighty God here on Earth. God wants you to begin to discover how valuable you are to Him and the strategic role you play. We as children of the Highest must begin to understand that God wants to use us. God did not create us just to live here on Earth and know Jesus as the Savior of our souls. Yes, Jesus is our Savior, but we must understand that there is a whole lot more to God's plan for us after we are brought into the Kingdom of God.

Guess what: God did not create you just because He was bored and needed someone to fellowship with. There is much more.

Before there ever was a you, there was a plan for your life and a problem for you to solve for God throughout your days. We must begin to understand the importance of our existence. It doesn't matter to God how you got here. The reality of the matter is that you are here. You are not a mistake. Your life was skillfully planned out by a God who loves you dearly. Even if you were born to a mother who wasn't expecting you, you're here now, and God knew you were coming. We serve an all-knowing God who allowed you to enter the world for such a time as this. God wants to accomplish greatness through your life. He wants to use you to positively affect your sphere of influence in your generation. You have a divine connection to this planet you were born on. Let's dive right into some things.

"And the Lord God formed man of the dust of the ground, and breathed into his nostrils the breath of life; and man became a living soul."
Genesis 2:7

Let's take a look at the above scripture. According to Genesis 1:1, we know that God created the earth. In the above scripture, we see that God made man from the same material that He created the earth. That's very important. We must understand that God has an assignment for us to do.

The very fact that we were created from the dust of the earth shows that humankind has a direct connection to God's creation called planet Earth.

"God is a Spirit: and they that worship him
must worship him in spirit and in truth."
John 4:24

We as human beings consist of three parts. We are spirits who live in bodies, and we possess souls. One's spirit can be used as a gateway for God so that He may use us to fulfill earthly accomplishments. We need to look at this step by step.

"For in him dwelleth all the fullness
of the Godhead bodily."
Colossians 2:9

The above verse is referring to Jesus. Jesus is the mirror image of God the Father. When Jesus walked the earth, He was Emmanuel, God with us.

"Behold, a virgin shall be with child,
and shall bring forth a son,
and they shall call his name Emmanuel,
which being interpreted is, God with us."
Matthew 1:23

Just as Jesus was God on Earth, so are we to be, in a sense. Christ is our prototype. Christ is our pattern and our supreme example. Jesus was an extension of God. God had a yearning to affect the direction of mankind, so He stepped into a body in order to have access to us. Jesus was Emmanuel, God with us, as previously mentioned. Can you see that God had need of a body in order to come among us to accomplish things here on Earth? Jesus was used by God to solve a major problem. That was the problem of sin. Because of Jesus, many were and are being brought from a life of death into a life filled with God.

"For as by one man's disobedience many were made sinners, so by the obedience of one shall many be made righteous."
Romans 5:19)

Even satan understood the potential of the earthly vessel who went by the name Adam. Adam yielded his body to satan by allowing his earthly vessel to obey an instruction other than God's. This caused the earth and everything in it, including mankind, to change. Do you now understand the power you have on Earth to make a difference for God? Even one ordinary person can drastically change so much on a large scale on this planet. God wants to use your earthly vessel to make a major difference. God and satan desire to make use of your earthly vessel to affect the earth. What you carry out through the actions of your body can have a major effect on the planet and cause a major difference for mankind. This information should cause you to think twice about the actions that you plan to carry out. Are you allowing God to influence your actions or the devil? Selah.

Therefore, Jesus refers to us as the salt of the earth. People, we must understand our role and responsibility while on this planet that we are attached to. God wants to use us to make a positive difference for Him. God wants to use you to be a problem solver. We are called to be a light that shines the way to an intimate relationship with God. We are the salt of the earth.

"Ye are the salt of the earth: but if the salt have lost his savour, wherewith shall it be salted? It is thenceforth good for nothing, but to be cast out, and to be trodden under foot of men."
Matthew 5:13

"Ye are the light of the world.
A city that is set on a hill cannot be hid."
Matthew 5:14

God wants to use you to change the lives of people who are on a collision course with hell. Will you allow God to use you to impact lives on this planet? God is counting on you to be a solution for His glory and not your own. God has a master plan for your life and the life of everybody that you come across. With our human bodies, we can have a major effect on hundreds of lives. There are many people in the world affecting thousands of people negatively. God wants to use us on a grand scale to make a major difference.

In Christ dwelleth the fullness of God, as mentioned in Colossians 2:9. What does that statement mean to the body of Christ? In Christ dwells the entirety of God the Father. But the scripture says that the fullness of the Godhead is in Christ, bodily or in the body of Christ. If Christ is the head of the church, who is the body? The church is the body of Christ, so that means that the fullness of God is accessible to the church because of what Jesus did. Through the church, the fullness of God is manifested in the earthly realm, with Christ being the head, as the Bible does state that Christ is the head of the church. Take a moment and think about that. God, through Jesus, has built an organism called the church, by which He can demonstrate His fullness with Jesus being the head of it all. Glory to God in the highest! Isn't that awesome? So, under the leadership of Jesus our Lord, we have the legal right to manifest the fullness of Father God. And by releasing God in the earthly realm, we become problem solvers for Heaven. The church of God is the people, and the people are fleshly vessels that work together to create the church through which the fullness of God can be released.

Are you getting the revelation?

Will you release the fullness of God in the earth for God? The body of Christ, or the church, being self-aware means that we will understand that the plan of redemption was not just designed for us to get saved and go to church. Because of Jesus, the fullness of God can be released through earthly vessels as we yield ourselves to be used as tools by God and not satan.

"And he (referring to Jesus) is the head of the body, the church: who is the beginning, the firstborn from the dead; that in all things he might have the preeminence. For it pleased the Father that in him (Christ) should all fullness dwell..."
Colossians 1:18-19

What does it mean for Christ to be the head of the church?

To say that Christ is the head of the church is to say that He is the core director of the church. In every human being there exists a brain. With our brains, we receive information. The information that is in the brain is carried out in the body. Every directive is timed and sent to the body by the brain. Think about it– where would you be without your brain? First of all, without the brain, there is no life. And beyond that, there would be no direction or course of action. You as a human would be motionless and good for nothing. Information comes to our brains through our senses. Then, our brains process the information and tell us what to feel and what action to take based on how they perceive the information. We act according to how we perceive things, and the emotions we feel for any given circumstance depend on how we perceive what we are seeing. This is why people can experience the same thing but produce different emotions. This is why one hundred people can hear the same message preached and all of them can come up with different emotions and thoughts. It's not always about what is being said but how a thing is being perceived. This in turn elicits certain emotions.

Let's deal with the subject of perception for a minute.

How do you perceive the call and the destiny God has for your life?

If you don't perceive the call of God to be important, you take it lightly. You tend to slack up on your reading and prayer life. You don't see the importance of attending church regularly, and fasting is out of the question. And when you receive a prophetic word, you easily forget about it. This occurs because your perception is off. At the same time, you go to work early and stay late. There is nothing wrong with having a career, but everything should take a backseat to the will of God for your life. Your perception governs your entire life, and your perception will determine the actions you will take. How do you perceive the plan of God for your life? Is it first and foremost to you?

Father God, in the name of Jesus, I pray for the reader's perception. I pray that the perception of Your chosen ones would mirror Heaven and destiny. In Jesus' name I pray. Amen.

"Take heed therefore how ye hear: for whosoever hath, to him shall be given; and whosoever hath not, from him shall be taken even that which he seemeth to have."
Luke 8:18

The above scripture refers to how you interpret what you have heard. Your interpretation molds your actions. If you don't take the right actions, it's because you perceived or interpreted what you've seen the wrong way. That is why the word of God tells us to be careful how we hear because if we take the wrong actions, we must understand that we can fall prey to being demoted in relationships in the world and in the Kingdom of God, as well as in the spirit realm. So, please be careful how you hear.

But what does all this have to do with Christ being the core director of the church?

The church without Christ being head is like the body without the brain. Christ perceives the will of God for the church through what God has shown to Him. And the actions of the core director, who is Jesus, are carried out through the function of the body of Christ, the church of the living God. Jesus is the brain of the church and its very foundation. He is the chief cornerstone. With the Holy Spirit, who is our Helper, we carry out the plans of the Master.

Even though Christ is the head, full of direction and purpose from God, He needs a body to carry out what's in His thought process. Everything that should be carried out from the mind of God on Earth is implemented by the headship of Jesus and is carried out in the body through the help of the Holy Spirit. What we see carried out by the church are the intentions of God on Earth! Isn't that awesome? We should perceive things differently regarding being used by God after a statement like that.

Are you excited about being a problem solver for God?

We must allow the perception of Jesus to be ours and not have our own perceptions about God's will for our lives. In the very mind of God are solutions to life's problems and dilemmas. These solutions have been delegated to the head of the church, which is Jesus. These solutions must be carried out in the body. God uses the church to release His thoughts in a flow of action with the aid of the Holy Spirit. Church, we must allow ourselves to be a gateway for the Kingdom of God to begin to invade Earth. There is a blueprint, a heavenly mirror image that the Father longs to see on the earth.

God wants to invade our problems through you. Are you ready?

The Father wants to use you to establish Kingdom blueprints, order, and structure on Earth. If God wakes you up early in the morning to pray for the nation, it's not in vain. God is using you to impact a dying world. You are a gateway. I charge you in the name of Jesus to receive strength to do the works of God in the earthly realm! I release the fire of the Almighty God to strengthen you now in Jesus' name. Amen!

Isn't it exciting to know that in spite of all you go through, you are birthing out a solution to someone's dilemma? Be refreshed in knowing that the work you do does not go unnoticed. People may not notice it, but Heaven does, and someday you will receive reward for partnering with God. Get excited– God has ordained you to be a carrier of answers for someone's problem here on Earth.

"And it shall come to pass in the last days, saith God, I will pour out of my Spirit upon all flesh: and your sons and your daughters shall prophesy, and your young men shall see visions, and your old men shall dream dreams: And on my servants and on my handmaidens I will pour out in those days of my Spirit; and they shall prophesy..."
Acts 2:17-18

Do you see what's really going on in the above scripture? We tend to always look at the fact that God is going to pour out His spirit. But what role does man play in the above scripture? What takes place in the above scripture is a result of God filling man with the Spirit, which happened prior to the above verse. In Acts 2:1, God filled man to spread the Holy Spirit across the earth. So that means we play a role in the fulfillment of the prophesy mentioned above.

"We then, as workers together with him, beseech you also that ye receive not the grace of God in vain."
2 Corinthians 6:1

When God birthed the church, it was always His will to use the church to aid in what He wanted to accomplish on the earth. Remember that God is Spirit, so He needs a body to release the action of His will.

When Jesus walked the earth, He demonstrated to us how God felt about sickness. When you manifest God in different situations, it causes the world to see how God feels about a thing.

"How God anointed Jesus of Nazareth with the Holy Ghost and with power: who went about doing good, and healing all that were oppressed of the devil; for God was with him."
Acts 10:38

Let's look at the above scripture. The scripture states that God anointed Jesus with the Holy Ghost and power who went about doing good. The entire reason God trusts us with His power is for us to do His works and bring glory to Him. The anointing is not for showboating and building a name for yourself. God wants to do good through your yielded, consecrated life. The anointing on your life causes you to be fruitful in Kingdom works. This is the purpose for the anointing– for us to be fruitful on the earth.

"Even so every good tree bringeth forth good fruit;
but a corrupt tree bringeth forth evil fruit."
Matthew 7:17

"Ye have not chosen me, but I have chosen you, and
ordained you, that ye should go and bring forth
fruit, and that your fruit should remain:
that whatsoever ye shall ask of the Father
in my name, he may give it you."
John 15:16

The point that I endeavor to make to you is that we must be bearers of good fruit; we must understand that we were called to do so according to the above scripture. As long as you are on the earth, it is your duty to be fruitful. God has set the church up with the responsibility of being outpourers of the very heart and nature of God. You have no other assignment as long as the earth remains in the state that it is in except to distribute the power of God. We are called to serve with the power of God. So, don't get caught up on titles; get focused on being fruitful. Only Christ-like character will cause your fruit to remain.

Let's get back to Acts 10:38. What picture does that scripture paint about how God feels about sickness? First of all, the scripture tells us that Christ was going about doing good. What was so good about what Christ was doing? He went about doing good, healing all who were oppressed by the devil. The picture that God showed the world when Jesus walked the earth was that He is a God that heals and that He has the ability to heal any disease. God showed the world through Jesus that He was bigger than sickness. Did you understand that? God used Jesus to demonstrate how He felt about sickness by using a clay vessel to act out what was in His heart and mind. God wants to use you to show the world His heart. God wants to use you as an expressed image of His thoughts. Jesus took a thought from God about sickness and showed the world God's heart about sickness. When Jesus healed people in His midst, He literally demonstrated to the world by His actions and said, "This is what happens when God comes in contact with sickness." What an awesome revelation about the thoughts of God. God doesn't simply hate sickness; God also wants to demonstrate that He hates sickness by using clay vessels. Since we now know that God hates sickness, take the authority over the demon behind sickness in your life and the lives of others and tell sickness that it is hated by God and it must leave your body.

Another important fact according to Acts 10:38 is that sickness is satanic oppression, so we need to understand that there is an unclean spirit behind sickness. Be a problem solver for the King of Kings and the Lord of Lords. God is raising up a generation of warriors who will demonstrate His power. God wants to show the world His face, and He wants to use you to do it.

Why does God want to use you to be a solution?

The reason is because He passionately wants to solve problems through you. God enjoys defeating the kingdom of darkness through clay vessels. By the Spirit of God, I know that God gets a kick out of that. I hope you're not too religious to receive that, my brothers and sisters in God. God, by His spirit, is always setting up situations to bring people out of the bondage of satan. God wants to use you in the workplace, in the grocery stores, at the department stores, and at the malls to demonstrate His heart. The call of God on your life is directly tied to a certain people that He has ordained for you to bless through the expression of Him in you. One thing you must understand is that, yes, you are anointed, but it goes beyond just you being anointed.

It's not about you!

The primary reason you are anointed is because God is thinking about somebody else. Did you get that? Let that revelation soak in a moment. Selah! God did not anoint you for you. God anointed you because He was concerned about someone else who is living outside His will. God wants to use you to save a gener-

ation of people from destruction. God is looking to you to partner with Him. God does not
anoint us to be served but instead to serve humankind. Never forget that we are Earth agents,
anointed and appointed to serve the people on
this planet. We are called to express God's attributes and to give the world a glance of God.

We must learn to get excited about someone
other than ourselves. We must begin to develop servitude. When God poured time and effort
into investing His glory in you, you must understand that He was passionately concerned about
the pain of another. That is why He raised you
up: to help someone other than yourself. Think
about it– when you were in bondage, God raised
someone up to aid in your deliverance. And now
that God has you, He wants to use you to do for
someone else the same thing He used someone
to do for you.

"Many will say to me in that day, Lord, Lord,
have we not prophesied in thy name? and in thy
name cast out devils? and in thy name done many
wonderful works? And then will I (Jesus)
profess unto them, I never knew you:
depart form me, ye that work iniquity."
Matthew 7:22-23

Please make sure you look at the above scripture carefully. What is God trying to say to you? The nature of the anointing on your life is to bless someone other than yourself. Your relationship with God is yours alone to maintain. The anointing on your life does not negate the fact that you still must press hard into God for intimacy. We cannot allow gifts to make us think that we are in a safe place. In the Kingdom of God, so many people are drunk on their own gifts. We can't allow our walks with the Lord to slack. Even when you are used heavily by God, you still have to maintain connection in His presence. We must not allow a gift we have to entice us out of right balance and relationship with God. We must remain disciplined to seek God's face. We cannot get relaxed because we walk in a certain manifestation of God's power. In the above scripture when Jesus said, "I never knew you", He was talking about intimacy with God. He was saying, "Yes, you were anointed to do works for me. But I never knew you. You did not take time to strip yourself of your gifts and come away with me."

Oh, people of God, we must understand that gifts will not save you but rather others. Can you handle being gifted and maintain relationship with the Father at the same time? Or will you allow yourself to be seduced by your gifts and the call of God on your life?

"Give, and it shall be given unto you;
good measure, pressed down, and shaken together,
and running over, shall men give into your bosom.
For with the same measure that ye mete withal
it shall be measured to you again."
Luke 6:38

You see, we always tend to religiously look at what will be given to us, but we forget that we must give first and that God uses man to give. But in understanding that God uses us, we still must maintain sanctification. Yes, God uses us, but we can't let our marriages and relationships fall by the wayside. We can't even allow ministry to become an idol. We must understand the nature of the anointing. Did you know that the anointing has a nature of its own? The anointing is designed to go out and bless, help, and work. However, if you don't watch it, you can lose balance. And what started out as a work for God can ship-wreck you if you don't maintain a pure balance. Know that God uses man, but more than that, know that your relationship with God must not go neglected.

"But I keep under my body, and bring it into
subjection: lest that by any means, when I have
preached to others, I myself should be a castaway."
1 Corinthians 9:27

Even as anointed as Apostle Paul was, he still had to maintain integrity behind closed doors, not just before people on a platform. Let's go back and touch on why we are anointed. During this portion, please read Exodus 1 and 2.

In Exodus 1, the children of Israel have come under bondage by Pharaoh. The children of Israel begin to multiply to the point that the Egyptians are intimidated because they realize that the Israelites are outnumbering them and are mightier than they are. So, the pharaoh over Egypt makes a decree that all of the male infants should be killed. During the time that Pharaoh made the decree, Moses was born. God did not allow Moses to taste death. God caused Pharaoh's daughter to have compassion on Moses. She raised him as her own child in the palace under Pharaoh. After the child was reunited with his mother, the mother of Moses received wages for nursing her own child. How awesome is that?

"And it came to pass on those days, when Moses was grown, that he went out unto his brethren, and looked on their burdens: and he spied an Egyptian smiting an Hebrew, one of his brethren."
Exodus 2:11

At this point, Moses began to manifest the deliverer within. He rose up and killed the Egyptian who was afflicting the Hebrew. Moses discovered that the news got back to Pharaoh. Pharaoh sought to kill Moses, and Moses fled from the face of Pharaoh.

Let's stop here for a moment. You need to understand something. All that was going on in the life of Moses was for a specific reason. There was a reason that the life of Moses was abruptly interrupted. Hold that thought!

"And they said, An Egyptian delivered us out of the hand of the shepherds, and also drew water enough for us, and watered the flock."
Exodus 2:19

You need to see something here. Know at this point that while in exile from Pharaoh, Moses comes across seven daughters whom he helps to fetch water. In the above verse, they call him an Egyptian. But we know that Moses is Hebrew and not an Egyptian. Think about that. Moses' identity has not been revealed to the world yet. Until you answer the call to solve a problem here on Earth, until you understand your assignment, until you go through the process of birthing, you don't have an identity. Your identity to mankind and the Kingdom of God is rooted in the problem you are called to solve! That is why every time you hear the name "Moses", you hear the word "deliverer". The word "deliverer" is in the identity of Moses, so everyone associates him with that word and the phrase, "Moses the deliverer". To bring deliverance to the Hebrews was what he was anointed for. It was his problem to solve. Being a deliverer became his identity because that was his function on this planet.

"And it came to pass in the process of time, that the king of Egypt died: and the children of Israel sighed by reason of the bondage, and they cried, and their cry came up unto God by the reason of the bondage. And God heard their groaning, and God remembered his covenant with Abraham, with Isaac, and with Jacob. And God looked upon the children of Israel, and God had respect unto them."
Exodus 2:23-25

The above scripture sets a stage for a particularly important revelation. Why did God bother Moses in the first place? Why did the life of Moses turn upside down in a moment's time? Moses went from Pharaoh's palace to being exiled. Are you ready for the answer?

In Exodus 2:25, God has respect for Israel. Also, God hears the groaning of the children of Israel in Exodus 2:24. There is a progressive revelation we must look at here.

The Answer

The only reason there is an anointing on your life is because God is passionately concerned about the groaning, crying, and bondage of the world. Remember you are an Earth agent. For God to ease the pain on the planet, He needs ambassadors to go on His behalf. He needs a body that can dwell on the earth. God can't do that since He is Spirit. We are Earth-dwellers. We have something to offer God. Isn't that awesome? God gave us His only son to save us. Now we have a chance to do something for Him. The very fact that I can do something for God excites me. How about you?

Getting back to Moses...

The children of Israel were in bondage, and God wanted them out, so God raised up an Earth agent that He could flow through to accomplish a task. God needed someone to deal with a problem, the problem of bondage and mistreatment of God's chosen people.

That brings focus to your life. Understand that you are called to destroy satan's kingdom, not just in general but a specific part of his kingdom. Moses was called to be a great deliverer. He led Israel out of Egypt through the wilderness and to a place where Canaan was in view. Who do you think Moses did all that for? He did it for God. Selah!

Can you picture the dialogue between God and Moses?

Use your imagination for a moment.

Picture this:

God would say, "Moses, I have a problem."

Moses would ask God, "God, what's Your problem?"

God would reply, "My people are in trouble. They cry unto Me night and day. Will you go help them for Me? You see, Moses, I have this problem. I am a Spirit. I can't move around on the planet like you can. You know, Moses..." God would laugh and then continue, saying, "Since the Earth is My footstool and all, it would be kind of difficult for Me to help them. Moses, since you have a body, can you help Me?"

We must hear the cry of God to use us. God is yearning to use even ordinary you. One day, I was up praying, and God began to tell me something that shocked me to my core. God said to me that He is desperate to find someone to use. He said "desperate". There are certain things that can only be done by a human on this planet. First of all, I had no idea that God was even capable of feeling desperation. Secondly, we must understand the responsibility that God has given us to manage and steward the earth. What a high calling. We can't neglect it.

The above dialogue takes place one way or another when God calls someone to work for Him. Are you ready to bring solutions from Heaven to Earth? God would be ever so grateful. You must understand that it should be a pleasure to work for Him. That should make you think twice about disobeying the King's orders. You are called for a specific purpose, so get in the birth position!

Chapter 2

†

The Foundation

Before you can do anything for God, there is an area you must look at. It's time for you to consider your foundation in the Lord. How deep are your roots in God? The call of God on your life is likened to the Sears Tower building in downtown Chicago. The Sears Tower, now called the Willis Tower, is one of the mega structures of the world. Everyone is always walking by, snapping pictures, and gazing at its magnificent size and structure. Tourists come from all over the world to view the Willis Tower. Inside it, there is a lot of activity. This large infrastructure is just like the call of God on your life. How do you view your ministry?

Has God told you that He wants to use you to do something mega on Earth? Where do you see yourself in ten years? Are people going to come from all over the world to view what God has done through you? There are important Kingdom principles we can learn from the Willis Tower. The things of God are clearly seen by viewing the natural things that are on this planet.

"For the invisible things of him from the creation of the world are clearly seen, being understood by the things that are made, even his eternal power and Godhead; so that they are without excuse..."
Romans 1:20

It is part of my assignment from God to leave you without an excuse. The information I have been given from God for you has the power to point you in the right direction. It's God's will that you are prepared to walk in His call on your life without setbacks. God needs to deal with some things that are a part of the very core of your existence. God is an awesome God. It is so loving and caring of God to deal with some things in our lives while we are still in the foundational stages of fulfilling destiny in His Kingdom. You must remember that God is an all-knowing God who knows all things about you. He knows all your flaws. God also knows how the enemy seeks to destroy everything about you. This is not a joke. Let's get serious. I need you to meditate on the below scripture.

"Be sober, be vigilant; because your adversary the devil, as a roaring lion, walketh about, seeking whom he may devour..."
1 Peter 5:8

To be sober means to be reasonable, and to be vigilant means to be alert. There are some things that God must bring to our attention while we are still in the foundational stages of our lives in ministry. You see, the reason God must deal with us is that He does not want us to fall prey to the enemy. God wants us to walk in His will and not get tripped up by the craftiness of satan. Again I say, as I mentioned previously, that this is the love of God revealed to us. Because God loves you and can see down the road of your life, He chooses to fortify you. God deals with the problem areas of our lives so the enemy can't get in through the cracks. Despite all the things we endure in becoming saints, God does not want us to suffer as people caught in sin. God never intended for us to suffer defeat because of a lack of preparation that causes us to be open, easy prey for the enemy of our souls. God never intended for us to go that way. Hear God, beloved– don't suffer a breakdown because you did not allow God to properly prepare you. That is not the way!

"For it is better, if the will of God be so,
that ye suffer for well doing,
than for evil doing."
1 Peter 3:17

Who told you that you can secretly live a lifestyle of immorality and preach the gospel? If you are caught up in pornography, homosexuality, adultery, theft, fornication, or other sins, you need to take some downtime and get some healing. God never intended for you to live a double life. You need to get free.

Begin to rebuke the spirit of compromise. It just brings me to tears, powerful men and women of God getting caught up in secret sins. These things should not be. In this day and age, so many people in the church are getting exposed by the world and caught in sin. So many are being found to have private struggles with adultery. Men of God, get yourselves together. You cannot think you can walk in immorality and maintain credibility in the world. You will be found out. Yes, God will forgive you, but your witness is compromised, beloved. We must remain the salt of the earth.

You need to fall on your face and cry out to God for deliverance. Guess what: you need to expose yourself the right way before the enemy exposes you the wrong way. There should be someone in your life you can go to in order to get help.

Exposure breaks the back of the enemy and his grip on your secret area of sin.

Just think about it. Here you are day by day, going to church, shouting and speaking in tongues, and when you leave church, you're on the internet or other places caught up in immorality. I know this is raw, but somebody has to address this. This is love talking, not condemnation. God loves you and wants to keep you safe. This is all motivated by love. Inwardly, you really want to be free, but you can't get free from the clutches of the enemy. One main issue with young leaders is a lack of accountability. God does not want you to suffer alone! Please hear me and get some help. I've never seen so many prominent men and women of God falling because they gave in to the constant pressure of the enemy.

Remember we are still dealing with your foundation.

"Confess your faults one to another, and pray one for another, that ye may be healed. The effectual fervent prayer of a righteous man availeth much."
James 5:16

You know, we always quote the latter part of the above verse, but we forget about the first part. What we need to understand is that God honors us when we seek help. When we have private struggles and we make the decision to expose the enemy, God rains down His holy fire on us. Did you catch the revelation? God honors us when we run for help. Don't just run to anyone; let God lead you to the right person so the situation can be dealt with in a godly manner. It is the enemy who seeks to isolate you and cause you to be on an island all by yourself so that when you need help, you are trapped. Once again, that is why you need a leader to birth you out right into the ministry you are to walk in on the earth. You will see statements like that throughout this entire book. You are nothing without the right leadership. The enemy knows you don't really want to be free when you operate in so much secrecy. But when you expose your area of infirmity, the enemy packs his bags. He knows his hold on you is broken.

The Strategy of Satan to Break You

> *"And he shall speak great words against the most High, and shall wear out the saints of the most High..."*
> *Daniel 7:25)*

Let me say it again: you need to expose yourself the right way before the enemy exposes you the wrong way.

Satan's Touch

When you have areas of your life that are in need of deliverance, the enemy starts a process against you. You see, satan knows our weaknesses. satan facilitates putting people, images, thoughts, and even computer pop-ups in your line of sight. The enemy continues for a process of time to brainwash you with immoral information until he weakens your willpower. He stains your soul with residue. One thing you must know is that satan is doing this while at the same time he is hoping and counting on you not to expose him. You must understand that satan is a sizable opponent. We should not take him lightly. If satan knows that alcohol is not your weakness, he won't use alcohol. He will appeal to your area of weakness. He studies your bloodline. The enemy comes to you to see if there is anything in you that looks like him. The enemy wants to see if there is anything in you that belongs to him. The enemy is looking for familiarity.

"Hereafter I will not talk much with you:
for the prince of this world cometh,
and hath nothing in me."
John 14:30

When the enemy comes, he is looking to see if anything is in you that he can communicate with. When he sends a lust demon your way, satan is looking for something in your soul or your flesh to respond. So, if you struggle with something like lust, and someone else comes along with the same spirit, there is an inward communication. Literally, your weakness begins to talk with their weakness and the unclean spirit in the other person. That is how it is. The enemy can only appeal to your area of struggle. The enemy seduces people, causing conviction to be weakened. After a long period of seduction by the enemy, you start to give in, which in turn dulls your level of resistance. This is only done by wearing you out over a period of time. You sleep, and you dream ungodly dreams. All throughout your day, the enemy works on your imagination, giving you mental pictures that are contrary to the holy standard that God sets for your life, and you fall prey.

At this point, you need to begin to cover your thoughts and dreams in the blood of Jesus and begin to cast down every wicked thought and imagination rigorously.

"(For the weapons of our warfare are not carnal, but mighty through God to the pulling down of strong holds;) Casting down imaginations, and every high thing that exalteth itself against the knowledge of God, and brining into captivity every thought to the obedience of Christ..."
2 Corinthians 10:5

It is also extremely important that you begin to implement warfare strategies such as in the above verse as well as seek help and pray with someone who is seasoned in deliverance.

"Again I say unto you, That if two of you will agree on earth as touching any thing that they shall ask, it shall be done for them of my Father which is in heaven."
Matthew 18:19

End-Time Warfare Strategies from Heaven

In this season, God is literally downloading information from Heaven to us. This is the season that God is giving us new information to fare well against the enemy. Because the enemy in this hour has turned up the heat, the devil is a sizable opponent. We still must be careful not to underestimate him because satan is far beyond just being crafty. Do I need to paint a picture for you? Do you realize that satan studies you? When it comes to your downfall, satan is patient and persistent. The enemy will match your every move, just waiting for a moment of weakness so he can slip in and wreak havoc in your life. The enemy hates to see you wake up in the morning, especially if you are walking in destiny because God has called you to solve problems here on Earth that the enemy has caused. satan studies you. You are set directly against the very face of satan, and he hates you with a passion. The enemy hates God, you see, and that means he hates you, too, beloved. So, stay sober.

"Be sober, be vigilant; because your adversary the devil, as a roaring lion, walketh about, seeking whom he may devour..."
1 Peter 5:8

My particular call is to leaders and the next generation of young warriors for the Messiah. As leaders, we pour out and pour out, but who pours back into us? There is a different type of training and seasoning that we go through. You see, we are a different type of salt. There is salt for the preservation of mankind, and there is salt for the leaders. I am salt for leaders. I am a minister's minister by the grace of God.

Those of us who are called to be generals, upper ranking in the Kingdom, we must understand our opponent, satan. The devil strategically sets up bear traps and tactics against us. The enemy is not out just swinging at us hoping to hit a target. He is a strategic attacker and is targeted in his war strategies against us. Because the enemy is crafty about our destruction, we must remain yielded to the Holy Spirit. Yielding to the prompting of the Holy Spirit is an immensely powerful warfare strategy. In this hour, we must remain yielded to the Holy Spirit more than ever. Do not underestimate satan. You may say this information is not about the foundation. Oh, but it is! When your ministry begins to rise like a tall building, there is an intelligent host of hell waiting to knock you down. God must spend at least ten years on your foundation to prepare you to stand against the one who wages war against your soul– ten years at least.

"And I heard a loud voice saying in heaven, Now is come salvation, and strength, and the kingdom of our God, and the power of his Christ: for the accuser of our brethren is cast down, which accused them before our God day and night."
Revelations 12:10

Man of God, what is in your life that the enemy can go to God with concerning you? Women of God, is satan accusing you before God about your nasty attitude or your lack of purification? Take it back to the foundation.

I spent the last section talking about satan so that you can understand the need for a strong, solid foundation and you won't wonder why it's taken ten to thirteen years for God to birth destiny into your life. You see, there are so many ministries that have risen up, but certain areas of them are extremely questionable. Again, when you look at the height of the Willis Tower, you can understand that it must have taken a great deal of time and effort to lay the foundation. Just maybe you are a prophet to the nations. Maybe God is calling your ministry to rise high. Consider your foundation.

I can't stress it enough– we must, while we are small ministries, look at our foundation. What is holding the weight of the anointing on our lives? When you rise up in ministry, can what you've built stand against the spiritual earthquakes from the enemy that manifest in the natural? If God allows a shaking in your life, what will remain? Will your ministry fold? Did God really send you out there? How much pressure can the structure of your ministry take? Do not allow yourselves to be self-deceived; some of you are not ready yet. By the way, what's the rush?

Waiting On The Lord: Warfare Strategies

"But they that wait upon the Lord shall renew
their strength; they shall mount up with wings
as eagles; they shall run, and not be weary;
and they shall walk, and not faint."
Isaiah 40:31

Let's break down this scripture, but before that, I have to give you some information. The war strategies of Heaven are changing. Yes, they are changing. What happens when binding and loosing don't work? What I mean by this is that sometimes the enemy works in secrecy. I'm not trying to be mystical, but there are certain things that we as ministers should have in place in order to keep the enemy locked out of our lives. You can bind and loose all you want, but if you don't know how to wait on the Lord, you can be destroyed!

The very existence of your ministry depends on you being able to wait on God. What happens when what you believe God for doesn't show up in time? Will you lose your character?

The Mystery Test of Delay

You must understand that there isn't anything–
I mean anything– that is hidden from God's sight.
God can see so deep into you that He will begin
to bring flaws and unclean motives out of you
that will scare your socks off. "Wow, I didn't know
I was like that!" Does that phrase sound familiar?
God knows the part of you that you don't know.

What is the mystery test of delay? There will
come a time in your life when you will begin to
have faith and believe for things only to be denied. Please, you must get this. Let that soak in,
pause, and meditate on this. You will pray and
fast until you are blue in the face, and still nothing will be in sight. I mean nothing. You might
say, "You mean my loving Daddy God would do
this to me? Doesn't He want me to have it?" Yes,
your Daddy God will definitely hold things back
from you. And newsflash, He is not doing it to
test you. God is omniscient, or in other words,
all-knowing. He knows your downsitting and
your uprisings. He knows the way that you think.

Here is the mystery revealed: God delays
things to begin to kill some things that are in
you that must die. At this time in your life, you
will think that God is your worst enemy. You will
begin to declare, "Why is God trying to kill me?"

At this amazing time in your life in God, delay will take on the form of denial, and you will feel denied. You will begin to say, "God, why is it that everybody else has certain things? They are half as faithful as me! God, don't you know that brother Joe Flo is sleeping around with sister Duma Flache? And they're ordained, they have a car, they have everything they want, they have a house. God, what are you trying to do, kill me?"

And God will say with a resounding voice, "Yes, my beloved child, I'm trying to kill you."

God begins to deny things to bring up deep, embedded character flaws that you didn't know were there. All the murmurings and complaining, all the impatience and doubt. And the spirit of compromise will begin to die. Before these things die, they must first be brought up and then out. You see, there is no deliverance of a thing until there is first admittance. God, at this point, is using denial and delay to purge the very core of your methods. Somebody say, "Thank you, Lord, for working on me."

Women out there, let's rap.

This is why it's taking so long for you to get the husband you are believing God for. Faith delayed doesn't mean denied, sister. At this critical time, so many of you settle for less and end up in a deadly snare. You must not compromise and settle for less. Wait...I say wait...for the manifestation of the promise. Let's be real, my sisters and brothers, if it doesn't fit the profile, it isn't God. So, don't flirt with the devil. Don't you dare touch it. Wait on the right divine door and let God purge you. Let Him clean you out. Allow Him to qualify you to become a problem solver for Him. When you compromise, no good will come from it; only death will result. Stop fooling yourself. Sometimes, we trick ourselves into believing a lie. We anxiously step out into something before it's time and then have the nerve to ask God to bless it. Then, once we get involved in something, the anointing, vision, and voice of God begin to die. Now you want to cry out.

But daughter, but beloved son, God never intended for you to be in that place.

How did you get there? You compromised and settled for less. You see, there is a portion of us that believes God never intended for us to walk in a permissive will. But we must walk in the perfect divine will of God. If I myself compromised, I can lose everything – my ministry, my marriage, my covenant relationships, and even my sanity. It's all or nothing for me. There is no compromise. If I were to choose another path, there is only death waiting for me. So, I must move out only by the voice and unction of the Most High. If I move out before God, I can lose everything. God help us. Compromise is death for you. Don't fall prey to temptation. It is not worth it. Cry out to God and ask Him for strength.

This is why waiting on the Lord is warfare strategy. You must discipline yourself to the point of no compromise. We must wait on the Lord because when God denies some things, it is only for our protection. Did you hear that? God is holding back certain things that you desire to protect you against your own downfall. Whatever God is holding back, there is a birthing getting ready to happen. And you don't want to have to deal with a premature birth. A lot of people miscarry because of lack of ability to carry full-term. They get nervous and try to help God and cause birth defects in their ministry. Allow God to birth you out and always remember it's not about you.

Let's go back to Isaiah 40:31, "Those who wait on the Lord shall renew their strength." What is God saying to us? This portion of the scripture is directly tied into vision. As you minister to the Lord like a waiter in a restaurant, you receive something. When the scripture is talking about waiting, it is not suggesting that we sit around idly. That scripture suggests that you should become a waitress or waiter in the Kingdom of God. That means while you are ministering to the Lord in prayer and obedience, He'll begin to pour out vision as you wait. Hallelujah. Let's wait on Him. When Daddy God sees that you are waiting on

Him, He begins to bless you with insight and vision. Along with this vision comes the ability to mount up, run, and not be weary. The vision that God pours out causes you to soar like an eagle with wings far above everything in your present situation that does not look like the fulfillment of promise. You literally can see things a different way. You gain insight to see beyond the lies of satan. You mount up into another realm full of hidden treasures of information. When you don't wait on the Lord, there is no insight, and you begin to settle for less. It's easy to settle for less when you don't have the vision of the best. You don't believe anything is coming, so you say, "What's the use? Why wait?" You step out in the flesh, and the end result is that you begin to miscarry the call of God on your life. Do you see how important waiting on God is? You don't have to stay in a low place of blindness. Wait on the Lord, and you can soar to the mountaintop of revelation.

Let's mount up.

Don't try and create opportunities out of haste. When you do that, you'll have to maintain false opportunities in your own strength without God's grace.

Hear me, saints, we must learn this during the foundational stage of ministry when God is laying the cement or foundation to do a work for Him. Waiting on the Lord is a powerful warfare strategy because when the enemy of your soul begins to present things to you that are not from God, you won't just accept them. In this type of situation, binding and loosing won't work. You need to stick to what you know the promise of the Father is. Don't let compromise cause you to miss God. Your adversary – the devil – is intelligent. Guess what: he hopes you never know that. If satan can get you to believe that he is just a dark, angry cloud floating around, he knows he has you because you won't really be looking for him to be so strategic to your demise. So, begin to wait on God. Allow Daddy God to flood you with a picture of destiny so that when satan presents the wrong thing, you can know that thing doesn't belong.

Satan Knows How to Attack Your Lack of Vision

"Where there is no vision, the people perish..."
Proverbs 29:18

The devil knows when you are seeking God and not your own way. When the enemy knows you are not seeking God, he begins to buffet you with half-truths like he did Eve in the Bible. "Thou shall not surely die!" When you are waiting on God and you are anxious, you need to know that the enemy uses that against you. That is why, beloved, you must stay in the Word and in the presence of God. Wait on the promise of the Father to manifest and don't settle for less.

> *"I will stand upon my watch, and set me upon the tower, and will watch to see what he will say unto me, and what I shall answer when I am reproved. And the lord answered me, and said, Write the vision, and make it plain upon tables, that he may run that readeth it."*
> *Habakkuk 2:1-2*

In the foundation-building season, we must set ourselves in a place of intercession, but on a higher scale and a higher grade. It's time to be planted in a place of birthing out the vision of the Lord. You know, given the way of the world, with all its new technologies and inventions, many have entered into a "microwave" season. There isn't anything you can't get in a moment's time. But we as Kingdom-builders must remain in a place of waiting on the Lord.

Get in the Birth Position

We must continue to be found in the presence of the Lord. If you are looking for me, I'm found in His glory, in the secret place of the Most High! Let us stand before Him in the birth position, ready to hear what He has to say. We can't allow ourselves to get caught up in a "popcorn" mentality. Some things take days, months, or hours to birth out. Your furtherance in the will of the Father depends on it. In order to catch the moves of God, we must remain in prayer. Selah. You can't keep up with God outside of Him. Did you hear that? I repeat: you cannot keep up with God outside of Him. Turn off the television and go to bed. The functions of your day should be centered around the time you spend with God, not the other way around. It's time to reorder our days. You know, we give God the time we have left over. When you begin to give God the first fruits of your day, He will honor you with vision to move ahead.

But without the vision of the Lord in your life, you are stuck at a red light. And you will miss God if you move forward on a red light.

What does it mean not to settle for less? Sometimes, you compromise the vision God gave you for your life, thinking it's okay and saying, "God won't mind if I stray just this once." You need to really get that. Newsflash! Whatever you compromise the will of God for, no matter how big it appears to your flesh, it's really less than the perfect will of God for your life. Though it seems like a great big opportunity that will never come around again, you see, God may tell you, "Don't go to that big church engagement. Go to the storefront church across the tracks and minister life." To the flesh, going through the big door to stand on the big platform looks greater than. But it's really less than. Anything outside of God's will is less than. So, let's not allow our fleshly ambitions to trick us out of the will of God. Let's get something straight: God always has our best interest at heart. God is not some producer trying to dupe and deceive you and squeeze out of you every opportunity to get ahead. But let's hear the balance of the thing. It's not about creating a name for yourself, anyway. Jesus didn't do that. The fame that Jesus received was a direct result of him staying in the will of the Father. Becoming well-known just happens, but when you get into a place to try to market yourself, you'll just miss God.

Habakkuk 2:1-2 covers information about the position of intercession and vision along with running forward.

When you don't get the vision, you don't have direction. You become stuck at a red light. You can't run without vision. We must learn early on in ministry that we cannot get ahead of God. You must be sure of one thing: when you move on a red light and you don't have a "go" in your spirit, you might as well get ready for a car crash in the spirit.

What a mess.

You must understand that when God tells you, "No, not right know", it's for a reason. God is looking out for your safety. Listen to God, beloved. Don't move until you get the vision and timing. Your life depends upon it because there are some things you might not recover from. We must be quick to obey the promptings and guiding of the Lord. When God begins to impress on us a certain thing, it behooves us to listen. God does not disturb us for nothing.

"Take fast hold of instruction; let her not go; keep her; for she is thy life."
Proverbs 4:13

Let's look at the above scripture. The word of God talks about instruction being our life. What does that mean? The scripture tells us to grab hold of instruction for it is our life. What if somebody told you that they were losing the ability to breathe and that they would soon die? It's the same with instruction according to the scripture above. That means that without instruction, you will die. You may not experience natural death, but God's original plan for you will start to wither or fall away from you. Your ministry will die, and the mantle on your life will lay dormant, which will only lead you to have a form of godliness but no real Kingdom expression. To be a problem solver for God, you cannot lose your breath. You cannot lose instruction from God. That means to be in perfect balance, you need to have God's instruction for your life. Without instruction, there is suffocation. Do you now see how essential it is to receive direction? The instruction of the Lord literally keeps your Kingdom expression alive. If you want to be a problem solver for God, you have to receive God's instructions. The reason instruction escapes us is because we don't want to spend enough time seeking the Lord, ministering to Him in prayer and sitting in His presence long enough until we become saturated with His Holy Spirit. We must learn to full up with Him like never before.

"It is the spirit that quickeneth; the flesh profiteth nothing: the words that I speak unto you, they are spirit, and they are life."
John 6:63

When you receive the instruction of the Lord, you must understand that you receive your life source– for the health of your ministry, your life, and everything else that your life consists of.

What is the reason we need our flesh to eat a well-balanced diet?

We eat in the natural for nourishment. We eat in the natural to remain healthy.

When you rob your body of food (apart from fasting), your body is void of nourishment. Without nourishment, you don't have strength. Sooner or later, you will begin to waste away and perish.

We feed our flesh three hot meals a day, but we feed our spirits a cold snack on the way to work.

To remain strong and fortified, we must feed our spirits. We as God's children must understand spiritual diet. What table are you eating from? What are you eating from the table? This is an important factor to learn while we are in the foundational stage of ministry. We must discern our spiritual diet. Begin to ask God what a healthy spiritual diet looks like. Too much candy will rot your teeth.

Don't let anyone fool you with sweet, sugary prophecy. Learn to discern the motives of those speaking into your life. Begin to discern why people are in your life. God puts people in your life for you to bless them or for them to bless you. Don't just let people come in and out of your life. Begin to seek God for the purpose of other individuals.

When a mother gives birth to a child, that child is immediately put on a special diet. There are stages at the birth where feeding is extremely critical. For the baby, there is a formula selected that is full of nutrients. The essential nutrients in the formula cause the child to grow up healthy and without any deficiencies. If the formula is lacking any essential minerals, the growth of the baby is affected. After the baby is on the formula for a while, the baby graduates to a higher level of food or a different type. The diet changes along with the growth of the child. Can you imagine if the child were drinking straight carnation milk?

Our growth should be monitored like the above statement. We must have the right diet or formula to grow correctly. When the child grows a bit older, the child is ready for solids. But we must also understand that a baby does not have a system that is mature enough to digest a steak. Through the study of the Word and by submission to leadership, we become ready for strong meat and are made able to digest strong meat.

While you are young in ministry, your diet is essential so that you may produce healthy ministry with the right balance. Stop for a moment, pray, and ask God to show you what healthy ministry looks like. When you digest a healthy diet, you will be able to recognize healthy ministry. The reason we see unhealthy ministry growing rapidly is because of the diet the leaders grew up on. It's even possible that the leader started with a healthy diet, but they allowed seducing spirits to lead them down the wrong path.

Through the study of the Word and prayer, healthy ministry is produced. But we must understand while our ministry is young how important diet is. You are what you eat. Allow God to feed you the carrots and peas of ministry through good leadership. Don't let your craving for notoriety and creating a big name for yourself seduce you. The awesome thing is that good diet is habitual. When you allow yourself to be raised on good diet, you develop a taste for it. Because I sat under a good ministry where the Word went forth, there are certain things I just can't listen to. Once you develop a taste for the meat of the Word, you tend not to just be tossed to and fro by every wind of doctrine.

"For when for the time ye ought to be teachers, ye have need that one teach you again which be the first principles of the oracles of God; and are become such as have need of milk, and not of strong meat. For every one that useth milk is unskilful in the word of righteousness: for he is a babe. But strong meat belongeth to them that are of full age, even those who by reason of use have their senses exercised to discern both good and evil."
Hebrews 5:12-14

Study the above scripture carefully. Even when you develop a good diet, you still need years to grow. Sitting under good ministry of a pastor for just a few years won't cut it. Be like a tree planted!

How does the situation above occur? When you don't put the word of God into daily application, you begin to lose out. In other words, God will not allow you to operate on a meat diet until you live what you are being taught. When you don't live out the word of God, you are demoted to the milk stage.

"For every one that useth milk is unskilful in the word of righteousness: for he is a babe."
Hebrews 5:13

To be a problem solver for God, you must keep a healthy diet. Make sure the word of God is being put into action. Walk out God's plan for your life because talk is cheap. Being of age concerning spiritual matters means walking out the word of God.

Chapter 3

✝

DISCIPLESHIP

*"Herein is my Father glorified, that ye bear
much fruit; so shall ye be my disciples."*
John 15:8

To be used of God, it is most important that you understand discipleship. The term "disciple", according to Webster's Dictionary, is defined as "a person who believes in and helps disseminate the teachings of a master". What an awesome definition. So, according to Webster's, you have to do more than just follow to be a disciple.

According to the original Greek, a disciple is a pupil and a learner. What we are seeing is that a disciple is not just a person who attends church faithfully. A disciple is a person who can learn and retain what has been taught, and not just learn but be able to disseminate the things learned to people. "Disseminate" means to be able to spread and teach what's retained. That gives a death blow to the spirit of religion. No longer should you go to church week after week. No longer shall you talk about how good the sermon was and forget what you heard. Religion teaches us to go to church and get our emotions stirred, then go home, get drunk, smoke, curse, live, and be happy.

No, beloved of God. Get it together.

It's timeout for thinking we can be anointed and live any kind of way. Don't you see? That is why exposure has hit the church. God is no longer winking at our compromise.

"And the times of this ignorance God winked at; but now commandeth all men every where to repent..."
Acts 17:30

What the church got away with in times past shall be no longer. God is commanding the saints to walk the straight and narrow. If you want to be a problem solver for God, you must live holy. Holiness causes us to be a conduit for the Kingdom of God. When you begin to compromise your walk with God, you cause blockages. We must live clean lives, church. God is not looking for career churchgoers, people who attend church but do not attain Christlikeness. Let us move from a place of deadness into a place of function, going forth in the power of the Kingdom of a God and His subjects. In order to be a problem solver for God, you must be able to become what you are taught. Become what you are taught! When you become what you are taught, you must begin to multiply yourselves in others. It's about spreading the Kingdom.

The Great Commission

> *"Go therefore and make disciples of all nations,*
> *baptizing them in the name of the Father*
> *and of the Son and of the Holy Spirit..."*
> *Matthew 28:19 NKJV*

Let's look at the above scripture. Jesus released the twelve disciples to spread the gospel. According to the New King James Version, the disciples were commissioned to go out and make disciples of all nations. Can you see the spreading of the Kingdom of God in the above verse? So, what the Word is saying is go spread salvation, then bring forth maturity so that the people just recently brought to God can go out and begin to reproduce. God is changing the face of the church.

It's not about just teaching and preaching. It's about raising up sons and daughters who can begin to have spiritual children of their own. That means that church leaders don't have a right to lord over the people of God and tie them down. Leaders, you don't own the people of God. They are the sheep of His pasture. It's your job to raise up and send out. It's our job as fathers in ministry to bring our spiritual children into a place of functioning in the call of God on their lives. Again I say, God is changing the face of the church. Selah.

What Are We Doing With Precious Ministry Time?

Those of us who are pastors and overseers of churches, are you really being effective? Are you a good steward over the great commission? Are you really answering the call? Time is precious. What are you doing with it? Are we truly spreading the gospel of Jesus Christ?

In this hour, we must be timekeepers. We must watch the length of time we spend accomplishing Kingdom business. We must begin to measure the length of time against effectiveness and faithfulness. Are we faithful in the time we spend? Are we productive?

Length of Time x Effectiveness = True Disciples

It is my solemn duty and God-given purpose to stress the subject of discipleship. Discipleship is the heart cry of the Father. With mine own eyes, I see great men beginning to fall from a place of witness to the world. I've seen great women compromise their chasteness. We cannot just let the enemy come in and disqualify us from experiencing God's best. We must safeguard ourselves against the wiles of the devil. We must understand that even though satan understands that his time is short, he is persistent. The enemy of our soul is picking away at areas of our lives, mostly areas that we have not allowed God to process. The enemy is a master at using us against ourselves. This is no new strategy, but satan has turned up the heat. We must understand that satan is pure evil. He wants to snatch your witness. He wants to snatch the influence you have gained through your process. He wants to snatch the very life of the call from you! How would you act if you knew that someone were standing outside your door with a pistol? Would you just brazenly walk out the door? I don't think so. You would attempt to ambush the ambusher.

Guess what: the key to ambushing the one who is attempting to kill the anointing on and in your life is discipleship. Can you understand how that is? This should be speaking volumes to you.

"And there shall be signs in the sun, and in the moon, and in the stars; and upon the earth distress of nations, with perplexity; the sea and the waves roaring; Men's hearts failing them for fear, and for looking after those things which are coming on the earth: for the powers of heaven shall be shaken."
Luke 21:25-26

For years, we have heard that we are in the end times. But never in history has the atmosphere given signs of the times like now. Global warming and destruction by water are happening like we've never seen before. There are tsunamis and earthquakes and tornadoes in unheard places. Lately, you could barely tell if it's summer, spring, or winter if it weren't for a calendar. Now you tell me if we are closer or not to the coming of our Lord. This is a progressive revelation. I am going somewhere with this.

I have paid the price for what I'm about to say. The reason so many leaders are falling away is because of the end times. The church leaders of the past can't handle the pressures of the present. Yes, there is nothing new under the sun, but the old schemes of the enemy are coming at a great level of force and craftiness. Never has the enemy challenged our integrity like now. Never before has there been such pressure from the enemy. Never before have we seen so many leaders caught up in chasing filthy lucre. Never before have we seen so many leaders given to homosexuality being exposed. We have great men of God preaching an all-inclusive gospel that everybody on Earth is already saved. Things are not the same as twenty years ago or even ten years ago. Never before have we seen so many leaders given to pornography. It's extremely easy to sin these days. It's time for a reconditioning. The victories of the past cannot sustain us today.

It's time for the church to transition into discipleship and begin again. Time to become a pupil, a learner, and a disciple afresh.

Dear Eli and dear Moses, the training you received in yesteryear is not enough this year. Your level of resistance is not strong enough. Your level of purification is not pure enough. The times we're in call for a deeper intake of inventory.

It's time for the elders in ministry to transition into a deeper conditioning. Become pliable again and be refreshed and refueled so you can hate what the Father hates. Come out from the world and be ye separate!

If you don't transition, the Kingdom influence you have will be ripped from your hands like it was from Saul's. Leaders of old, it's time to be regenerated with a washing from the word of God.

It's time to get in order again and be retrained to withstand the pressures of today. It's time to understand severity in the Kingdom of God.

Elis and Moseses, can your reputation handle it? Can the name you built for yourself submit to a refreshing? If all the fathers fall, we are in trouble.

The Sin of Eli

"Now Eli was very old, and heard all that his sons did unto all Israel; and how they lay with the women that assembled at the door of the tabernacle of the congregation."
1 Samuel 2:22

A telltale sign that you as a leader have compromised your walk with the Lord is when your sons in ministry become immoral and you allow them to stay in office. Somewhere in Eli's life, he was compromising his work with God, and it was telling in the offspring he was producing. That means something inside Eli liked what his sons were doing. Watch this: Eli himself was not said to be doing what his sons were doing, but for him to allow them to stay in office shows that Eli certainly got a kick out of what his offspring were involved in. Let's look at the picture. Eli was living out his fantasy through his children.

"Lay hands suddenly on no man, neither be par-
taker of other men's sins: keep thyself pure."
1 Timothy 5:22

"Now the sons of Eli were scoundrels who had no
respect for the Lord or for their duties as priests."
1 Samuel 2:12-13 NLT

Now, how is it possible for Eli's sons to be in such a state with he himself supposedly being the head? Just think about that. Compromise caused Eli to relinquish his influence, and he became dull.

Transition into Discipleship

Eli allowed certain things to take place in his presence so that over a process of time, his level of resistance diminished. Therefore, he was no longer convicted.

"Be not deceived: evil communications
corrupt good manners."
1 Corinthians 15:33

Who's in your inner circle and what type of lifestyle are they living around you? Does their level of sanctification challenge you to stay pure? Or is your resistance being torn down?

We Must Watch the Manifestation of Carnality

A big sign that we are caught in carnality is in the people we call friends. If I want to get to know what kind of a person you are, all I have to do is look at your friends. What are you attracting? Did you understand that?

It's time for men and women everywhere to understand deeper levels of purification. Discipleship and purification go hand-in-hand. You cannot go higher in God and into the manifestation of purpose without allowing God to begin to break things off your life. Let's look again at the friendship situation.

There came a time in my life when God began to cut away certain relationships. Certain issues and sin began to surface. It got to the point where I began to be irritated to the tenth power. I began to become disgusted with my own self. What caused this deep disgust? Being in the presence of a holy God!

Please understand it was not that God shunned me or looked down on me. But we must understand that God is a holy God. That will never change, no matter how much you cry about how much you love God. You will at some point have to deal with His holiness. There was a time in my life, one year in particular a while ago, when I lay before God for hours. And I still do. You can't remain in the presence of a holy God without it affecting your life. You see, that's how I know that Jesus is the Christ, the son of the living God. There is not another religion on this planet that produces pure change towards peace. I know Jesus is the Christ because my life has changed. I don't struggle with certain things anymore. I don't have to wear a "church face" and be harboring a secret identity or struggle. It is only Jesus who offers deliverance. It is only Jesus who brings true liberation, causing us to love the unlovable, causing us to experience days of Heaven on Earth in the midst of chaos. Christ offers lifestyle, not religion.

As I said before, there was a time that God released me, in that I lived and breathed His presence. As I got closer and closer to God, things began to surface in my life. You see, when you are in the presence of His majesty, the only person you are going to see for a long while is your own self until He can trust you with the lives of His sheep.

Gold goes through a process of purification. When gold is being processed, it is subjected to intense heat until all impurities surface. And when the impurities begin to surface, they are scraped off the surface of the gold. Then the gold has to be molded into a certain shape in order to serve a certain purpose.

We must go through the same process.

God will not put you on display until you go through a purification process. This process takes place numerous times in our lives, as we grow closer to God. Now, as God began to purify my life, I felt kind of good for a little while. Then, God began to deal with my associations.

Let's face a hard truth. When you've reached certain levels in God and you keep company with others who are caught in a lifestyle of sin, what are you doing? You are still feeding off corruption. There is something in you that is trying to desperately hold on to your past sin nature.

You must let it go.

What you are really saying is, "Just in case I want to dip back in a little, I have the right sin associates." Then we try to use the excuse, "I'm trying to save them." If you are trying to save them, why have you not brought your past friends around your saved friends? It's because you know that once your pastor meets them, he or she will see directly into your other identity. If you can't say amen, just say ouch!

"Be not deceived: evil communication corrupts good manners."
1 Corinthians 15:33

We've looked at the above scripture once already. Let's go back and break down the word "communication". Now, we all know that the Bible's original languages were Hebrew for the Old Testament and Greek for the New Testament, right? Let's look at the original meaning for the word "communication". "Communication" comes from the Greek word homilia, meaning "intercourse". So, if true communication refers to intercourse, and you have corrupt associations that you keep on a leash, what's really going on? Now let's look at the revelation about intercourse.

What is God saying about evil communication or evil intercourse? What happens when you just have conversations with people who indulge in sin?

When you are communicating with people who have sinful lifestyles and put them on a friend level, something happens. Remember that word "intercourse". Understand that in the Kingdom, you are on a course. When you feed unclean soul ties, it causes things to "enter your course" that don't belong, things that you are letting into your life to taint you while on your discipleship course.

"Wherefore seeing we also are compassed about with so great a cloud of witnesses, let us lay aside every weight, and the sin which doth so easily beset us, and let us run with patience the race that is set before us."
Hebrews 12:1

Have you ever seen a horse race? Have you seen those horses thundering around the track with the people in the stands screaming and cheering them on? Have you seen the great cloud of witnesses looking from afar as they run? Take a minute and picture yourself as one of the horses in your mind. You are running along, trying to fulfill the mandate of God on your life. Picture the horses running again. Suddenly, one horse crosses over into the path of another horse and trips, bumping the other horse and causing a chain reaction. Now, all the horses along with the jockeys begin to tumble and fall going at top speed, causing broken bones everywhere and death to some.

This is what happens when you allow perverse relationships to continue when you reach certain levels of purification in your life and in God. God loves us dearly, far beyond what we can imagine. He wants to shield us. He wants to safeguard us. We must cut the enemy off by closing doors. Sometimes, doors are wrong associations. The enemy seeks to cause a train wreck in your life. Never have I seen so many ministers fold as in this day. What's happening? Let me apologize if this seems harsh. That's not my intent. The Bible teaches us not to make occasions for the flesh to cause us to fall.

Because you might not deal with certain issues in your life, you think you get by. That is, until twenty years down the line when you have a ministry, and the enemy begins to pick at a sore spot in your life and cause you to give in, then exposes you like he's been waiting for years to do.

You must deal with purification now or deal with a mess later. It's up to you.

In these end times, we cannot handle both sin and the anointing. We are coming to a time when ministers with secret lives will begin to fall dead right in the middle of Sunday's sermon. God is not going to allow it. Look how God is exposing the Catholic church.

"For the time is come that judgment must began at the house of God: and if it first begin at us, what shall the end be of them that obey not the gospel of God?"
1 Peter 4:17

A Heart for the Lost

In this hour, God is calling us to have hearts for the lost. Ministry is not an avenue to pimp the world. We must be concerned about reaching the lost by being gateways to the glory of God. As mentioned in past chapters, we have to qualify ourselves to be gateways. God wants to release an anointing to heal the sick as seen in Bible days. But God is looking for the trustworthy. Who can God trust with His power? Can God trust you to remain focused on the mandate that's been given to you? Or will you allow filthy lucre to taint you? What motivates you? Why do you do what you do? God is calling for the genuine to come forth! God is calling for the genuine to walk in end-time anointing because we are in the end times and we must be pure at heart. We must have hearts for the lost.

"Pure religion and undefiled before God and the Father is this, To visit the fatherless and widows in their affliction, and to keep himself unspotted from the world."
James 1:27

God is calling for a genuine anointing, real and authentic, not hypocritical but sincere. God is calling for ministry that produces results. Real ministry produces results. When you come across a tree that has no fruit in a season when it should, there is a root problem.

What type of results are being produced in your ministry?

Let's take a look at James 1:27. This verse talks about visiting the fatherless and the widows in their affliction.

When you operate under a genuine anointing, you have a compassion for people in their affliction. This entire book is about being a problem solver for God. The true anointing of God stirs your heart to a place of action and to the production of results. Remember Moses. The passion he had pushed him to action. Moses could not stand to see the brutalization of his people under Egyptian rule. So should be the anointing on your life.

What is the sign of true anointing?

True anointing will not allow you to remain unburdened in the presence of the oppressed.

When you don't have compassion for the despondent, something is wrong.

"And Jesus went forth, and saw a great multitude, and was moved with compassion toward them, and he healed their sick."
Matthew 14:14

If you find yourself restless in a good way, if you have a burden for a problem in the earth, know it is for a reason.

You Have Compassion Because You Can Solve The Problem

Why would God unsettle you about a problem in the earth and not give you the ability to solve it? God is a complete God. It would be torture for God to give me a heart for leaders and their problems and not give me the solution. The reason you can't sleep at night and you're restless is because God eagerly wants you to discover the solution and then allow the genuine anointing on your life to make a difference in the earth.

In Matthew 14:14, it states that Jesus was moved with compassion. That means that Jesus went from a motionless state to a place of function. The compassion inside of him drove him to action. The entire reason he was compassionate about the multitude was because there was something in Him that could make a difference.

It was a genuine anointing.

If God is not unsettling you about things regarding the earth realm, maybe it's because you don't qualify to solve the problem. The only reason you wouldn't qualify to solve the problem is because you don't have a genuine anointing that produces results. The only reason you wouldn't have a genuine anointing that produces results is because God does not trust you with His power.

The only reason God would not trust you with His power is because you would use His power for fame and fortune. The only reason you would be in a place where you would abuse the anointing is because you wouldn't be allowing God to purify your heart and cleanse your motives. All of this takes place in the foundational and discipling stages where one learns to deny themselves, go through the process, count the cost, and pay the price.

Compassion exists in the heart of the qualified!

If Jesus were not at the place where He could be a gateway for healing, the condition of that multitude (referring to Matthew 14:14) would not have bothered Him at all.

Understand that the anointing is on your life to produce results. But let's talk about balance. One thing we must do is watch our ambition for ministry. When God is ready to promote you, He really doesn't need your help. He knows how to release favor and bring you out of hiding. Money should never be your motivation. God provides provision for His vision. God's will, God's bill. Allow God to make a way and don't try to do it on your own by demanding unreasonable support financially. Sometimes, we just need to take a step back and discern. Ask yourself, "Am I operating in fleshly ambition?" Don't get ahead of God. When God has great ministry in you, you must seek Him for divine provision. The only reason we fall into spiritual prostitution is because we have not tapped into God's pre-ordained plan for us to receive provision.

Just as much as we have vision for ministry, we must have vision from God concerning our needs being met. So, when you operate according to God's provision plan, you won't prostitute the gospel. You need vision to stay within moral jurisdiction concerning money; that way, satan can't tempt you to rob the saints.

This is where our faith kicks in, knowing that God has a financial plan for us. I can't stress this enough – accept God's plan for your care. Eliminate the opportunity or chance to get caught up in filthy lucre like it says in Titus 1:7. The phrase "filthy lucre" refers to when someone obtains financial gain dishonorably. I see so many pastors today over-accessing the people because of greed and fear of not being able to make ends meet. Those of us who are stirred with compassion, we cannot allow satan to trick us into robbing the church. You must have faith in God's provision. Check your morals, son. Check your morals, daughter of Zion.

You cannot operate in integral ministry while not having faith in God's provision. We must get this area right, people. This issue of provision is just as important as having compassion.

Take a moment and ask yourself, "Do I have God's plan for provision or am I depending on handouts?" Face the issue.

"For yourselves know how ye ought to follow us: for we behaved not ourselves disorderly among you; Neither did we eat any man's bread for nought; but wrought with labour and travail night and day,

that we might not be chargeable to any of you: Not because we have not power, but to make ourselves an ensample unto you to follow us."
2 Thessalonians 3:7-9

We must find the line of balance; we must learn how to handle God's people. You can't possibly have integrity going from church to church, robbing the church of thousands of dollars. How can you sleep at night knowing that a ministry is in a deficit because you ran a one-week revival?

Transition into Discipleship

In being ministers, we must be discipled into learning the purpose for the anointing. We must have a true picture of what it looks like to function with a genuine anointing. The below scripture is what it looks like to be anointed for real.

"How God anointed Jesus of Nazareth with the Holy Ghost and with power: who went about doing good, and healing all that were oppressed of the devil; for God was with him."
Acts 10:38

Get the picture!

Chapter 4

✝

LEADERSHIP

Let's get something straight right from the start: there is no ministry apart from leadership being in your life. Just as Jesus is the cornerstone of the church, so is leadership the cornerstone for ministry.

"Behold, I will send you Elijah the prophet before the coming of the great and dreadful day of the Lord: And he shall turn the heart of the fathers to the children, and the heart of the children to their fathers, lest I come and smite the earth with a curse."
Malachi 4:5-6

Before the return of our Lord the Christ, there will be a new anointing bursting on the scene. Selah! This new anointing is an end-time event that will take place on the earth. Take a moment to soak that in. This end-time event is a new fivefold grace being released on the earth.

The above scripture prophesies the return of the ministry of Elijah the prophet during the end times right before the coming of our Lord (or rather His return).

Warning!

This revelation that is now being written about is a revelation that must be caught while being taught. You can't see this without the assistance of the Holy Spirit opening the eyes of your understanding. Before continuing, take a moment and pray the below scripture verbatim in prayer form. Then, pray in the Holy Ghost, go back, and start this chapter over, reading it out loud at a slower pace. You will then find your understanding opened.

"That the God of our Lord Jesus Christ, the Father of glory, may give unto you the spirit of wisdom and revelation in the knowledge of him: The eyes of your understanding being enlightened; that ye may know what is the hope of his calling, and what the riches of the glory of his inheritance in the saints, And what is the exceeding greatness of his power to

us–ward who believe, according to the
working of his mighty power..."
Ephesians 1:17-19

This new fivefold grace in these end times is creating a space for itself. It is my assignment from God to show you what this new grace looks like. Before God can begin to multiply this new leadership grace, He needs someone to introduce it. Manuals will be produced so that this new grace can be introduced to the body of Christ and then activated in the lives of the ones chosen to walk in this ability. I am sure I am not the only one writing about this new end-time grace being released. Above all, God wants the body of Christ to get the picture and receive this grace so that it may become a working, thriving ministry in the earth in multiplication.

Leaders in the Middle of Leaders

This new grace in times past may have just been a stepping stone leading in a different direction, but it is now becoming a functioning office in the Kingdom. This grace is designed to create a cohesiveness between senior leaders and leaders under leaders.

"That which hath been is now; and that which
is to be hath already been; and God requireth
that which is past."
Ecclesiastes 3:15

Please go back and read Malachi 4:5-6. The thing that explains grace is the spirit of Elijah. This old testament mantle is the new thing that is being released in the earth with a new function not seen in times past in a previous function. The spirit of Elijah that is now being released is a grace on a person that stands in between senior leaders and the leaders under them.

This new grace is a divine enablement that causes senior leaders and the leaders serving under senior leaders to relate and understand how each other functions and how they should work together. This new grace stands in between different leadership, and this grace will deal a death blow to the spirit of Jezebel trying to tear up our churches.

The Vision of the Lord

God showed me a vision. In this vision, I saw a man speaking. By the spirit of discernment, I could see that this man had an apostolic call on his life. This man was standing up, addressing others who were sitting and listening. As the apostle was speaking, the ones listening were unresponsive. God began to show me that the words of the apostle were of no effect.

The End of Vision

Afterwards, I began to seek God concerning the meaning. By revelation, God began to show me that there was a missing link in between chiefs and their captains. Then, God began to show me the scripture in Malachi 4:56. God showed me that this was the anointing on my life and that it would be introduced to the body of Christ. God said this information will be birthed into manuals and be taught and activated in Kingdom schools and churches.

I must admit that when God told me to write this book, I had no idea this information would surface. This vision came to me with instructions. This took place shortly after I met with my daddy in the spirit as He spoke to me about my function and role in the ministry. After we had that talk, God gave me the vision with a mandate, and then the spirit of Elijah sprang alive in my life, and a new ministry was birthed. I don't know all there is to know about this, but my mandate is to introduce this revelation and then walk in it and begin to activate it in others. I am sure I am not the only one who knows about this. God will begin to release this information in books, manuals, and churches worldwide.

Leadership

Whenever God is releasing a new leadership grace, it is to fill a need, a spot, or a void, and to solve a problem. This entire book is about solving problems here on Earth for God, who is in Heaven. This is my ministry and my problem to solve: to unscramble the miscommunication between leaders here on Earth.

This anointing is released to:

1. Create cohesiveness between chiefs and captains by releasing a grace to cause the captains under leaders to remain planted and not be uprooted by satan.

2. Create an excitement and compassion between chiefs and captains to walk together, causing them to fall in holy love one towards one another.

3. Unscramble the lines of communication between them.

4. Bridge the gap and remove the spirit of estrangement between them.

5. Remove the fear of fathering that causes terror in the hearts of leaders.

6. Remove the fear of being mentored from

the captains under chiefs.

7. Cause a knitting together of hearts.

The purpose of releasing this information and revelation is that this grace can be recognized in the church and individuals set aside for this work can begin to come forth. In this time, we must understand the necessity of strong leadership in our lives. As mentioned before, just as Jesus is the cornerstone of Christendom, so is leadership vitally important. There is no salvation apart from Christ. There is no success in ministry apart from good, solid leadership.

Parallelism

Leadership is as important to producing healthy ministry as Christ is to Christendom.

"Now therefore ye are no more strangers and foreigners, but fellowcitizens with the saints, and of the household of God; And are built upon the foundation of the apostles and prophets, Jesus Christ himself being the chief corner stone..."
Ephesians 2:19-20

Without Jesus, all is lost. Without Jesus, salvation is in vain, empty, and void. Without the foundation, which is built by the ministry of the apostles and prophets, ministry is vain, empty, and void. Without Jesus, the gospel is of no effect. Without solid, healthy leadership, your ministry will be of no effect.

"Wherefore also it is contained in the scripture, Behold, I lay in Sion a chief corner stone, elect, precious: and he that believeth on him shall not be confounded. Unto you therefore which believe he is precious: but unto them which be disobedient, the stone which the builders disallowed, the same is made the head of the corner, And a stone of stumbling, and a rock of offense, even to them which stumble at the word, being disobedient: whereunto also they were appointed. But ye are a chosen generation, a royal priesthood, an holy nation, a peculiar people; that ye should shew forth the praises of him who hath called you out of darkness into his marvellous light; Which in time past were not a people, but are now the people of God: which had not obtained mercy, but now have obtained mercy."
1 Peter 2:6-10

Just as God has laid Christ as the foundation for your life, you must understand that God has also laid chief leaders in your life to birth out the call of God you are to walk in. Leadership is the plumb line that sets the cement correctly. In times past, I experienced the wrong type of leadership, which altered God's plan and timeline for my life, causing the foundation of my ministry to be slanted. But God sent me to proper people, who reset the foundations of my life, causing me to be the man that I am today. God has allowed me to experience all types of leadership on every level, good and bad, so that I may qualify to fulfill the call of God on my life to be a go-between for people in ministry and leaders. This is my mantle, my function, my assignment, and my problem to solve.

Listen to me carefully. Just as the verses said above, the stone, which the builders disallowed, the same was made the head of the corner, the most important piece of the establishment. What mentor or leader whom God has put in your life are you disallowing to shape you? When you reject leadership, you stumble. When you reject leadership, that very thing becomes a rock of offense. Just as Jesus is a rock of offense to those who reject Him, that means the very thing that you rejected is the thing that will "keep you out" concerning healthy mentorship. In this hour, satan desires for you to shut up your heart and be offended, which opens the door to the bastard spirit.

The Spirit of the Bastard

Whenever you cut leadership out of your life, you become stuck at that point. You can't go on. You are deceived, thinking you are prospering, but you are not. Two years can go by, and you will still be at the same spot that you were in when you disallowed mentorship. Mentorship is God's way and God's system. You cannot get around it. You cannot disallow it.

Just like the scripture said previously, when you reject Jesus, you are appointed to a life of stumbling. The same is true when you reject God-given leadership. When you become transparent, mentorship begins. When you become open, mentorship begins to complete a work in your life.

Get the picture!

When you allow leadership to handle you, you are passed from level to level, faith by faith, and glory to glory. Proper leadership stands on both sides of the road to destiny underneath Christ.

Picture yourself as a 2-year-old being passed by a line of adults, one leader passing you along to the next level of growth. At the end of the tunnel is a light you will never reach if you don't allow leadership to pass you on. There is no passing unless you are passed through the arms of your daddy and mother in the spirit. Selah. If you don't get anything else I said, please get this. Where do you see yourself in ten years, five years, two years? If you want success in any of the above timeframes, then you had better see yourself passing through the hands of leadership for it is the only way to the light at the end of the tunnel. Leadership is called into your life to bring a right balance.

"A false balance is abomination to the Lord: but a just weight is his delight."
Proverbs 11:1

One of the key things leadership needs to accomplish in your lives is godly balance, but leadership cannot call you. The calling comes from God and is confirmed by leadership. Wrong, controlling leadership will attempt to block the call of God. At that point, you'll have to make three decisions. One, you must not become bitter. Bitterness will trap you and disqualify you for purpose by keeping you out of alignment. The anointing cannot flow through a bitter vessel. You will have to get deliverance and then healing after you forgive. You must forgive. Selah.

Secondly, you must start to trust again because to stay safe and keep a proper balance, you need a covering of spiritual parents. Thirdly, after recovering from being wounded, you must find that covering or spiritual parent. You will have to become transparent again. To become transparent, you must be healed. If not, the correct spiritual parent comes along, and you will view them as a threat because you have been wounded. The enemy will have given you a one-two punch, and you will be trapped with this wound. Do not blame God for what men put you through. Allow the Holy Spirit to help you through it. My wife and I have been through this. I'm not telling you to do something impossible but rather something I have been through. My wife and I understand the spirit of Elijah coming to turn the hearts of parents and children back towards one another.

We must understand that leadership is set up in our lives for our protection so that we may move in the call of God apart from danger. We can't let our natural reasoning get in between the work that God is doing in us when He brings correct leadership into our lives. I've seen so many people in the body of Christ with much potential rise and fall simply because we forget that leadership is in our lives for a reason. Without leadership, we become lopsided in the things of God. We become tilted in our character and our methods. We need leadership to remain balanced.

Sometimes, we allow our natural reasoning to cause us to feel threatened by mentorship. I used the word "potential" a moment ago. Guess what. Potential is unused ability. God uses leadership in your life to bring out the fullness of God. So, what happens when we don't allow leaders to fulfill their roles in our life? We then are released into ministry with drops of fruitfulness but never tap into the flow and main thrust and power we are to walk in. What a shame. It just breaks my heart. I knew a young man who had a call on his life like I've never seen. But this young man and his wife would just not allow leadership to mentor them. And to this very day, they are stuck while everyone else is passing them by. It's a shame to admit it, but they actually think that they are doing well. When you don't allow leadership to work with God to build the proper foundation for your ministry, you become self-deceived, thinking you're okay while all the while being off-balance. God's spirit will not always strive with men. God is longsuffering, sure enough, but don't think God will just keep chasing after you to fulfill His call. God will just say, "Next in line; step up, please." I can't stress this enough: just as Jesus is the cornerstone of your faith, so is leadership the rock that balances you correctly. The last twenty plus years of my life, I have allowed God to have His way with His leadership. Because of that, the spirit of honor dwells with me and my wife.

People, listen. You will not get anywhere without mentorship. You need someone to lead the way. You need someone to take you where you have not been. You need someone to scout out the road ahead to make sure it's safe. These are the blessings that we reap from fathers and mothers in the spirit. There were times in my life when leadership had to say some rough things to me that cut me to the core. But in my mind, I knew I needed it. Above all, I had enough God in me to stay planted and not allow myself to become uprooted in spirit and action. People would make fun of me because I was loyal. I did not even allow bad leadership to rob from me what I knew to be right in touching things of leadership. When I look at the church today, I see tragedy for so many people called to impact the world. That door is locked to them because they feel being accountable is being a "yes man". You don't have to agree with everything said by your mentor, but if you annul their role in your life, you are lost, my friend. And guess what, you will not even know it because you'll be blinded by your wounds.

Why does God want to teach you how to follow? There are things you must learn as a servant and follower so that when you come into your leadership role, you will know how to treat people because you were once there. This is a proven fact. You can always tell if a leader has been properly mentored by the way they treat people. When you find leadership being nasty to people, that's a sure sign of false mentorship. There was one pastor that I would go out to dinner with. I would be so embarrassed. If the waiter made one wrong move, he would cause a scene. Just terrible! When are we going to learn how to treat people? How can you be a hellion and get up in the pulpit and preach? How can you curse out your spouse and then go minister while everybody in your household is wounded? These things ought not to be as becoming saints.

Wrong Leadership

I can't talk about right leadership without exposing the wrong. I know what wrong leadership looks like having been in situations with false fathers as authority over me. God allowed me to experience wrong leadership for your sake, beloved. You see, this book is all about being a problem solver, and before you can solve the problem, you have to walk through the situation and gain the solution, which is what I gained on your behalf. Now, let me show you what false leadership looks like.

How To Recognize False Leadership

First things first: check your motives. Are you looking for someone to make your name great? Yes or no? When you look to make your name great, you get in the bed with a leader who has the spirit of the hireling. You are looking to gain wealth and fame, and they are looking to gain wealth and fame through you and the potential they see in you. This type of leadership doesn't care about your safety or if they slant the plumb line for your life, causing a crooked foundation. All they see in you is a gift, and they will let you go forth in pride and arrogance and won't bring correction to your life.

In your search for good leadership, ask God to reveal the dollar signs in the eyes of the false.

Another sign is that you begin to discern them making a fuss over you. At the same time, you know you're jacked up. Yes, you can sing, but you curse like a sailor. Yes, you can prophesy, but you are caught in pornography. Yes, you have a great smile, but on the inside, your heart is full of callous rage and anger.

Through discernment, you should first pray for an increase of discernment.

Discernment is found in the heart of the pure. When you are truly sincere, God will show you the true spirit standing before you every time. When you are in it for the wrong motives, you are blinded because you are not really looking for truth. You are looking for money. You are looking for a husband. You are looking for someone to manipulate and play like a fiddle.

"Beloved, believe not every spirit, but try the spirits whether they are of God: because many false prophets are gone out into the world."
1 John 4:1

Do Not Fall Prey

"I am the good shepherd: the good shepherd giveth his life for the sheep. But he that is an hireling, and not the shepherd, whose own the sheep are not, seeth the wolf coming, and leaveth the sheep, and fleeth: and the wolf catcheth them, and scattereth the sheep...I am the good shepherd, and know my sheep, and am known of mine."
John 10:11-14

While seeking, ask God to reveal to you the leader with the father's heart. Hear me. If your mentor, pastor, or shepherd has a father's heart, every action they will take with you will be carefully thought out. If they have a father's heart, they don't have to be perfect. You must understand that they are human, too, my sons and daughters. Furthermore, because you are human, pastor, that does not give you the license to act out of character and be malicious and dogmatic.

Oh, how I have experienced that. That drill sergeant mythology is not of God but of witchcraft and is earthly. That form of witchcraft is done through control and domination. With that type of leadership, they think they own you and use phrases like "my people".

Dear ones, don't get caught in that. You won't be able to bat your eyes without needing permission. Ask God to reveal the spirit of domination and control in the atmosphere so contrary to the spirit of love and liberty. Don't make the mistake of being too deep with this or you won't see the forest for the trees. Witchcraft like this is easily seen in the atmosphere and not in the face of a false leader. This is a simple revealing. If you get too spooky, witchcraft will be all around you and you won't see it.

You can also tell by knowing what your assignment is in the local body you are in. Don't be so quick to jump ship. Has God sent you there? If He has, get what He sent you there for and remain planted until you get a sure release from Heaven.

To remain planted means to remain Christlike and not be uprooted by the urge to retreat to a soulless place of offense, rage, and anger. Remaining planted is more than just sitting there. It's how you sit and what spirit you serve in. Remain planted in the fruit of the spirit. You are planted when storms begin to blow and you stay rooted in the word of God. You are planted when you stand in Christlikeness and don't allow your attitude to become otherwise.

If you obey the above, when you meet your father, you will hear the sound of the Shepherd in your ears through their voice. I will never forget it when I first heard the voice of one of my mentors. The sound of his voice went through my ears and down into the depths of my spirit. And I followed hard after God.

God wants you to become what you are sitting under. God wants you to begin to mirror your mentor as you grow and develop like a child does under his daddy. A young child in early learning stages only repeats what he hears until what he learns forms a vocabulary and personality of his own. The child will always have the attributes of his parents, no matter where they go in life or how old they become.

Leadership: Father & Son Meet

"So he departed thence, and found Elisha the son of Shaphat, who was plowing with twelve yoke of oxen before him, and he with the twelfth: and Elijah passed by him, and cast his mantle upon him. And he left the oxen, and ran after Elijah, and said, Let me, I pray thee, kiss my father and my mother, and then I will follow thee. And he said unto him, Go back again: for what have I done to thee?"
1 Kings 19:19-20

When you come across your father, you and he both will know it. What was Elijah's mantle saying to Elisha that caught his attention? Elisha left his natural mentors and followed the spiritual ones. When your rightful mentor comes into your life, he or she changes the course of your steps. God wants to use you greatly, but you need help getting there.

Let the search begin for the mentor that is due in your life. Both mentors and mentees must be committed to the relationship and the process, and both must be willing to learn from one another along the way.

CONCLUSION: MY PASSION

My heart is that leaders everywhere will be knit together. It is so much my ministry, my ability, and my every waking passion and joy to see chiefs and captains mesh that my heart aches when I see the shutdown and miscommunication between God's leaders. My job is not done, and I am not at peace until the fabric is strengthened between captains and their chiefs.

The miscommunication between leaders is my problem to solve, and since before I was formed in my mother's womb, I was ordained a problem solver. I have the solution. I have the answer, the mantle, and the grace to bring about a meshing.

In writing this book, the thrust of the assignment on my life has been revealed: to serve God's senior leaders and their captains through the laying on of hands, bringing healing to the wounds of chiefs and their captains, wounds caused by the spirit of miscommunication and breakdown, to be the bridge that leaders and captains cross over from both sides to meet in the middle through the gift of prophesy. This is all by the grace of Father God, apart from whom I can do nothing.

My prayer is that you discover the problem God wants you to solve here on Earth and then get in position to birth out the solution. We don't have forever, saints. Time is running out, and the Lord is soon to come!

"I must work the works of him that sent me,
while it is day: the night cometh,
when no man can work."
John 9:4

About The Author

PASTOR AND PROPHET DONNY BLUMINGBURG is a man of God who has been on fire for God since high school. Prophet Donny has a unique call to bring people everywhere into a place of pursuing God and the supernatural. Donny co-pastors with his wife of 19 years, Prophetess Pastor Angela Blumingburg. They Pastor a church called Image Ministries currently in Hammond, Indiana. Prayer, seeking God, and the Word of God guides everything they do.

Also Available from
J. Kenkade Publishing

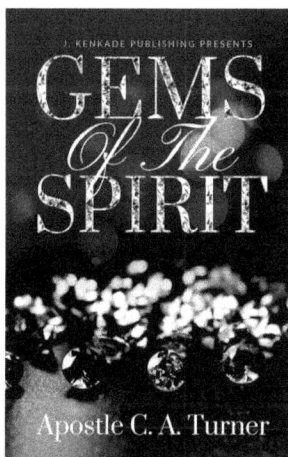

ISBN: 978-1-944486-83-9
Visit www.amazon.com
Author: Apostle C. A. Turner

There's such a hunger for the things of the spirit and the supernatural. Many have decided to tap into the dark side in order to understand more about the Supernatural and the things of the spirit. One of the reasons for this I believe, is because the church as a whole has lost the desire to see a move of God validated by his power with miracles, signs, and wonders. It's my desire and prayer that this information will activate you in ways you never dreamed as you apply it to your spiritual life.

Also Available from
J. Kenkade Publishing

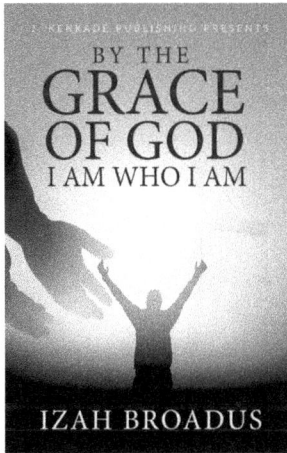

ISBN: 978-1-944486-58-7
Visit www.amazon.com
Author: Izah Broadus

Having seen death and having experienced multiple near-death occurrences himself, the author sets out to admonish and encourage others about a life that Christ gives that no street life can provide. After constantly watching so many young people and adults lose their lives to the streets and giving up on Jesus Christ, The Holy Spirit inspired the author to write this book to encourage others that there is hope in Jesus. From the streets to the pulpit, Izah helps others understand that the same God that helped him out of his lost situation is that same God that loves them as well.

Also Available from
J. Kenkade Publishing

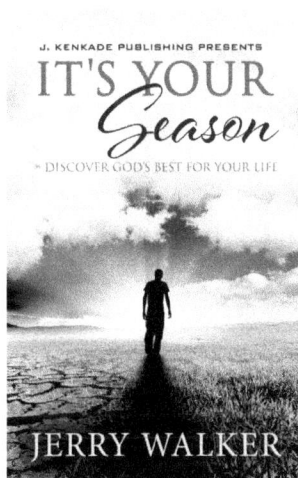

ISBN: 978-1-944486-51-8
Visit www.amazon.com
Author: Jerry Walker

Do you find yourself asking the question, "Is there more to life than the seemingly never-ending struggle of survival?" This book answers that question with a resounding, "YES!" Jesus died to give us MORE. Jerry Walker has written this manual for Christian living that gives in-depth teaching on scripture and how to apply it to your life. Full of tools for living a life of freedom in Christ, this book will be a blessing to all who read it. Your time is now, it truly is your season!

Also Available from
J. Kenkade Publishing

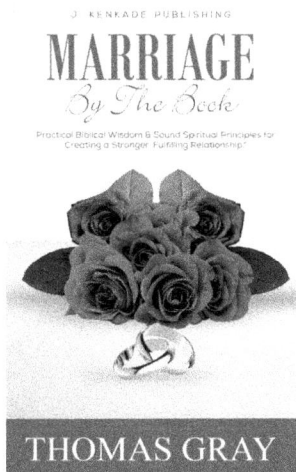

ISBN: 978-1-944486-90-7
Visit www.amazon.com
Author: Thomas Gray

Marriage by the Book is a profound and practical guidebook designed to help you cultivate a deeper relationship based on sound Biblical wisdom. Written by Pastor Thomas Gray, this book combines proven step-by-step strategies of practical relationships with spiritual lessons and Bible-based principles to help you overcome conflicts, improve your communication, handle difficult discussions, and celebrate the unique union and covenant which unites you together with God. Marriage by the Book is ideal for both new and seasoned couples who are searching for better ways to strengthen their relationship and fulfill their promises to God.

Pastor Thomas Gray: P.O. Box 360041/Dallas, TX 75336
www.twdcdaltx.org (972) 926-3762